VOCAL SELECTIONS
from
GEORGE M!

T0044811

Words and Music by GEORGE M. COHAN

There is a statue of him on the Broadway he loved at Times Square opposite the Palace Theatre where "George M!" made its brilliant New York debut. There is a tablet at the Table of Honor in the Oak Room of the Hotel Plaza, dedicated to him by the theatrical club "The Lambs," describing him as "The Most Brilliant and Versatile Gentleman in the Theatre of His Day." He is still fondly remembered as "The Man Who Owned Broadway." His career is known 'round the world through films, books, magazine stories and, above all, by the continued vitality and popularity of his songs. The "Yankee Doodle Dandy" was rewarded for his American spirit and songs when Congress voted him a special gold medal presented personally by Franklin Delano Roosevelt, whom he memorably played in "I'd Rather Be Right." However, the greatest tribute is the living portrayal by young Joel Grey in the successful "George M!" ... George Michael Cohan, song and dance man, always acknowledging the thunderous applause with "My mother thanks you, my father thanks you, my sister thanks you, and I thank you."

Contents

Illustrations Pages 36, 37, 73 and back cover

EDWARD B. MARKS MUSIC COMPANY

EXCLUSIVELY DISTRIBUTED BY HAL•LEONARD®

Give My Regards To Broadway

Words and Music by
GEORGE M. COHAN

Harrigan

Words and Music by
GEORGE M. COHAN

For I'm just as proud of my name, you see, As an Em-per-or, Czar or a King could be.
Thy la-dies and ba-bies are fond of me, I'm_ fond of them, too, in re-turn, you see.

Who is the man helps a man ev'-ry time he can? Har-ri-gan, that's me!_
Who is the gent that's de-serv-ing a mon-u-ment? Har-ri-gan, that's me!_

(Chorus) (Solo)

REFRAIN

H - A - dou-ble R - I - G - A - N spells Har-ri-gan.

(I'm A) Yankee Doodle Dandy

Words and Music by
GEORGE M. COHAN

10

Rose
(A Ring To The Name Of Rose)

Words and Music by
GEORGE M. COHAN

Revisions by Mary Cohan.

Mary's A Grand Old Name

Words and Music by
GEORGE M. COHAN

My Town

"I'm A One Man Girl"

Words and Music by
GEORGE M. COHAN

Revisions by Mary Cohan.

Nellie Kelly I Love You

Words and Music by
GEORGE M. COHAN

Musical Moon

Words and Music by
GEORGE M. COHAN

Revisions by Mary Cohan.

Oh, You Wonderful Boy

Words and Music by
GEORGE M. COHAN

Revisions by Mary Cohan.

So Long, Mary!

Words and Music by
GEORGE M. COHAN

Over There

Words and Music by
GEORGE M. COHAN

You're A Grand Old Flag

Words and Music by
GEORGE M. COHAN

Revisions by Mary Cohan.

All Aboard For Broadway

Words and Music by
GEORGE M. COHAN

Revisions by Mary Cohan.

The "stage family" featured in "George M!"
L. to R. Joel Grey, Bernadette Peters, Jerry Dodge, Betty Ann Grove

The Four Cohans at their height as troupers.

George M. an

Broadway's biggest producing team — Sam H. Harris and George M. Cohan.

Harvey Evans plays "Sam H." to Grey's "George M."

"Give My Regards to Broadway" sings "Little Johnny Jones."

"You're a Grand Old Flag" sings the "Yankee Doodle Dandy."

...re Broadway stars.

Father and son in one of George's plays.

The stage father, Jerry Dodge, buck and wings with "George."

Billie

Words and Music by
GEORGE M. COHAN

Revisions by Mary Cohan.

Musical Comedy Man

Words and Music by
GEORGE M. COHAN

Revisions by Mary Cohan.

Down By The Erie Canal

Words and Music by
GEORGE M. COHAN

Revisions by Mary Cohan.

All Our Friends

Words and Music by
GEORGE M. COHAN

Revisions by Mary Cohan.

Popularity

Words and Music by
GEORGE M. COHAN

Forty-Five Minutes From Broadway

Words and Music by
GEORGE M. COHAN

Revisions by Mary Cohan.

Twentieth Century Love

Words and Music by
GEORGE M. COHAN

Revisions by Mary Cohan.

Thom-as Ed-i-son, he's the one, who's be-gun ac-cel-er-a-ting; Now with Mis-ter Bell, Sam-'ll Morse___ as well, Why keep wait-ing.

No time___ to pitch woo now,___ The cen-tu-ry's new now,___
No time___ to pitch woo now,___ It's nine-teen-o-two now,___

Moderato two

Can't wait___ for that moon a - bove or e - ven a dove.___
No wait - ing for stars a - bove or e - ven a dove.___

So, kiss___ me and run, kid,___ It's nine - teen-o - one, kid,___
So, hur - ry to me, kid,___ It's nine - teen-o - three, kid,___

And I'm in Twen-ti - eth cen - tu - ry love!___
And be my Twen-ti - eth cen - tu - ry

love!___

Push Me Along In My Pushcart

Words and Music by
GEORGE M. COHAN

Revisions by Mary Cohan.

The Great Easter Sunday Parade

Words and Music by
GEORGE M. COHAN

Revisions by Mary Cohan.

I Want To Hear A Yankee Doodle Tune

Words and Music by
GEORGE M. COHAN

All In The Wearing

Words and Music by
GEORGE M. COHAN

Revisions by Mary Cohan.